Stand up and Walk
with
Jesus

AN ACTION RHYME BOOK

Stand up and Walk with Jesus

Leena Lane and Chris Saunderson

Pretend to open a door

Hurry! Hurry!
Jesus is coming!
Let's go in the house to see Jesus!

Hot! Hot!
It's crowded and hot!
Everyone wants to see Jesus!

Wipe brow with hand

Stand back! Stand back!
A man's coming down!
Down on a mat to see Jesus!

Stand back a bit to make room

Heave! Heave!
Lower him down.
Lower him gently to Jesus.

Pretend to lower a rope, hand over hand

Shake head and point to legs

Help! Help!
'Our friend cannot walk.
That's why we have brought him to Jesus.'

'Yes! Yes!
'Because you believed,
I will help your friend,' says Jesus.

Nod head and point

Published in the UK by Scripture Union

207-209 Queensway, Bletchley,

Milton Keynes, Bucks MK2 2EB

ISBN 1 84427 121 8

First edition 2005

Copyright © AD Publishing Services Ltd

1 Churchgates, The Wilderness,

Berkhamsted, Herts HP4 2UB

Text copyright © 2005 AD Publishing Ltd, Leena Lane

Illustrations copyright © 2005 Chris Saunderson

Editorial Director Annette Reynolds

Art Director Gerald Rogers

Pre-production Krystyna Hewitt

Production John Laister

All rights reserved

Printed and bound in China